WORDS and IMAGES

WORDS and IMAGES

Marcia Muth

SANTA FE

Cover Art: Marcia Muth, *Myr-Lou Park Zoo*,
from the Kaplan-Everhart Collection.
Cover Photograph by Carl Condit.
Author Photograph by Roslyn K. Pulitzer.

© 2004 by Marcia Muth. All rights reserved.

No part of this book may be reproduced in any form or by any electronic
or mechanical means including information storage and retrieval systems
without permission in writing from the publisher,
except by a reviewer who may quote brief passages in a review.

Sunstone books may be purchased for educational, business, or sales
promotional use. For information please write: Special Markets Department,
Sunstone Press, P.O. Box 2321, Santa Fe, New Mexico 87504-2321.

Library of Congress Cataloging-in-Publication Data:

Muth, Marcia, 1919–
  Words and images / by Marcia Muth.
     p. cm.
  Includes index.
  ISBN: 0-86534-438-8 (hardcover)—ISBN: 0-86534-437-X (pbk.)
  I. Title.
PS3563.U85W67 2004
811'.54—dc22
                    2004009519

WWW.SUNSTONEPRESS.COM
SUNSTONE PRESS / POST OFFICE BOX 2321
SANTA FE, NM 87504-2321 / USA
(505) 988-4418 / *ORDERS ONLY* (800) 243-5644 / FAX (505) 988-1025

For
Jody, Jim and Carl

CONTENTS

Foreword / 9

Part One
    People and Places / 12–45

Part Two
    The Drollites / 46–71

Part Three
    Other Creatures / 72–103

Index of Poems / 105

Index of Drawings / 107

FORWORD

I am often asked two questions. One is, "When did you start writing?" The answer is just as soon as I learned how to put words and sentences together. I loved words, ideas and making up stories. My first efforts were stories and essays. The stories were short and usually involved adventures and a generous amount of juvenile humor. The essays were requested by my grandmother who also suggested the topics. These were then read aloud by me to her friends who came in for afternoon tea. Looking back, I can see that these must have been boring interludes before the refreshments were served, but probably no worse than having to listen to someone's child playing a violin solo or the new piano piece. I can only remember two of the topics, "The Importance of Work" and "The Evils of Tobacco." Later, I began to write poems, mostly about nature. My interest in literature was stimulated by the first books I learned to read, school text editions of Shakespeare and Palgrave's Golden Treasury. It would add luster to the story if I could say that I deliberately chose those titles but the truth is that they were on the bottom shelves of a large bookcase in my room. I could reach them but had to grow before I got to the books on the top shelves. This bookcase was a treasure-trove of novels, history and old schoolbooks, some in French. They were from the late nineteenth century or early years of the twentieth but that didn't bother me. By my teens I had begun to send out poems and have an occasional publication. My writing career went happily on until ART became a serious contender for my attention. To the question, "When did you start to paint?" I say 1974. Actually, I had always had a secret desire to do some art, but after a few tries, I felt discouraged because I didn't seem to have a knack for it. In 1974, I bought some brushes, paint and small canvas panels. Once I took those first strokes, I never stopped. I started out by painting factories and other buildings and very gradually worked my way up to other scenes, people and animals. I also went to canvas and acrylics and then to ink and watercolor on paper. The more I painted, the more I learned. It has become the lodestar of my life. I am sometimes asked which artists I like or which ones have been influences. My favorites are Ben Shahn, Norman Rockwell and Edward Hopper. As an artist, I feel a kinship with all other artists from those who first drew on cave walls to those of today. We share a common legacy.

CREDO

I am an artist
I cruise the universe
Seeing faces
Selecting images
Like picking out apples
At any handy supermarket.
On a secret journey
I am a silent observer
Visiting neighborhoods
Collecting scenes,
There are no barriers
Between space or time
Everything is unfolded
Everything is understood.

PART ONE
PEOPLE AND PLACES

I have always been interested in people and places, the human nature and the human condition. As soon as I was able to read, I discovered the world as revealed in the local newspaper, not just the news, but advertisements, the comics and the myriad other attractions. Years ago, many newspapers also included in their daily offering continued stories and poetry. All of this, added to my personal observations, enriched my life and fed my imagination. Later that world would expand to include people and scenes from books and motion pictures. It stimulated my imagination to create my private world of people and places. I found that I had the freedom of a universal passport to go anywhere. There were no boundaries, no borders. While I shared life with real people, games with schoolmates and chums, I also had a secret life with a host of imaginary friends. As the only child in a household of adults, I was never lonely. Then I found I could bring some of those people and places to life by writing about them or drawing pictures. Although I started this as a child, I never gave it up and the end result has been poems, plays, novels (unpublished), drawings and paintings. To this day, the people and places in my work are imaginary. A good example of this is the poem that starts this section. I do not live by a river but one day I just knew what it would be like there. There is no drawing for the poem but the place is very real and clear in my mind.

THE RIVER

A river runs past my house
Sometimes noisy, filled bank to bank
Sometimes quiet, low and slow-moving
Always there and always changing;
It is my calendar of the seasons,
This river that runs through my life.

Now that it is summer, hot, sunny
The wide river swims with fish
Varicolored scales flashing, looping
In magical, enchanted patterns;
Above the water flying insects
Cling together in hanging clouds
That move along like balloons,
The deep sound of the Bach Suites
Comes from my neighbor's house
While two butterflies dance aloft.

In the autumn leaves fall and float
On the river's surface, going fast
Toward some certain destination
Like a thousand small offerings
Of thanks or beseeching prayers;
The last bird songs are heard
Frogs mourn the passing days,
Cicadas singing predicts winter
My neighbor now plays Elgar
And the wind whispers of melancholy.

Snow covers ground, trees, stones
Standing by the river, I listen
For the familiar sound of water
But the river is ice-bound now
Yet I know that under the ice
The river still flows sluggishly;
My breath-cloud mimics the sky
Overcast, a colorless cloudiness
Then I hear the music of winter,
Creaking of wood in the cold air
Sighing of ice as it forms and re-forms,
The crunching under fast-moving feet
Eager to return to house-warmth.

In the spring winter comes rushing
Down the river's usual course,
Fed by melting mountain snows
And early warm welcoming rains
Little clumps of green appear
All along the water's edge;
There is the joy and sweetness
Of many remembered tiny flowers
Now with windows and doors open
I hear Beethoven spilling out
From my neighbor's house and yard.

SLEIGHT OF HAND

Just as the magician pulls
The white rabbit from his hat,
Then a flowering bouquet
And scarves of many colors
That at a wave of his wand
Change to flying doves
So the composer amazes us
With notes blooming flowers
In the garden of our mind
That then like the doves
Whirl and fly freely
Across our expanded horizon.

BROTHERS AND SISTERS

The Daughters of Eve sit at the table
Playing cards, smoking, smiling
Nothing surprises them, even the comet
Sweeping slowly across the sky
They laugh at rumors of floods,
Fires, quakes, two-headed beasts
The whole panoply of disasters
All forecast by the sober
Sanctified Sons of Adam

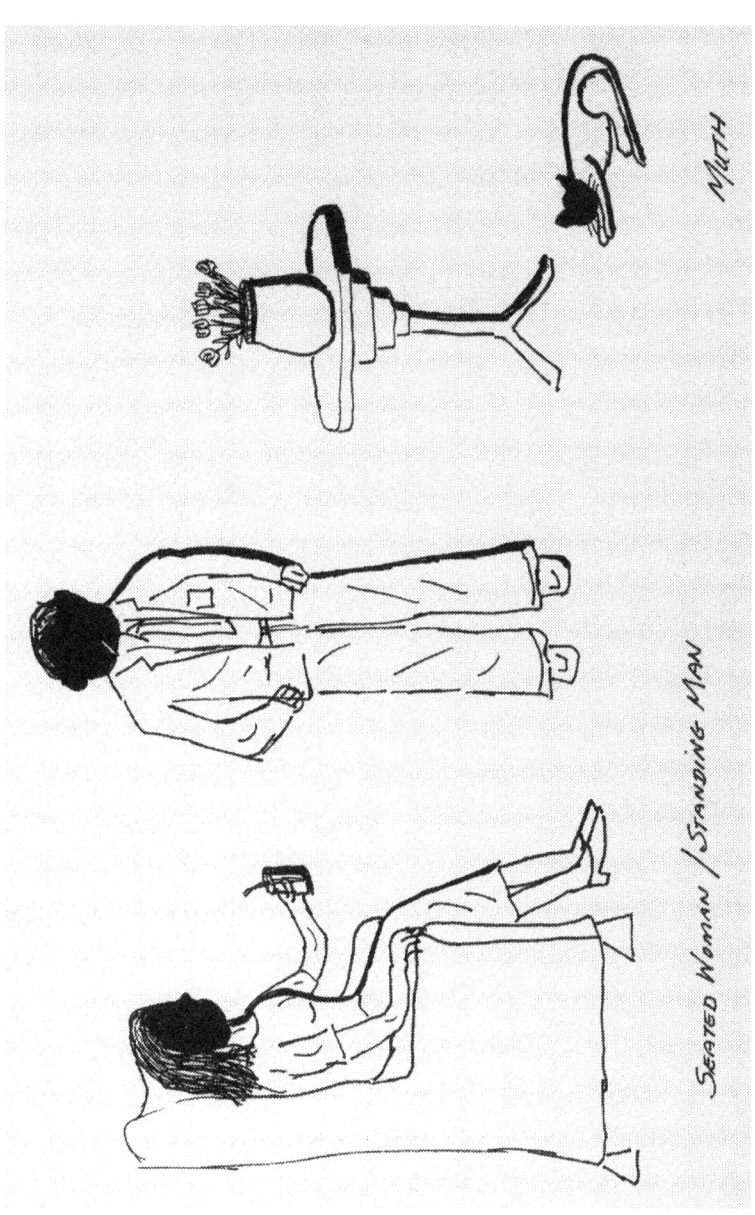

IN THE ROADSIDE HOTEL . . .

Sleepers turn uneasily
    Half-awakened
By highway sounds
    Dream-disturbed
By the rumble and clank
Of a passing freight train
    They wake briefly
Confused by the unfamiliar
Then still tired from travel
    hug tight
To their pillows for comfort.

Night Clerk at the Castaway Hotel — Math

SUDDEN RAIN

With the sudden rain
Umbrellas quickly sprout
Like darkened mushrooms

Rainy Afternoon — Muth

ICARUS REVISITED

In every generation
There is an Icarus
Who takes measurements
And plots his course;
Makes and shapes wings
To lift him far above
And once aloft, he flies
High and then higher
But just before the goal
Is reached, the day-star
Flames out against him
And he falls back down,
Twisting and spiraling
In an unforgiving sky.

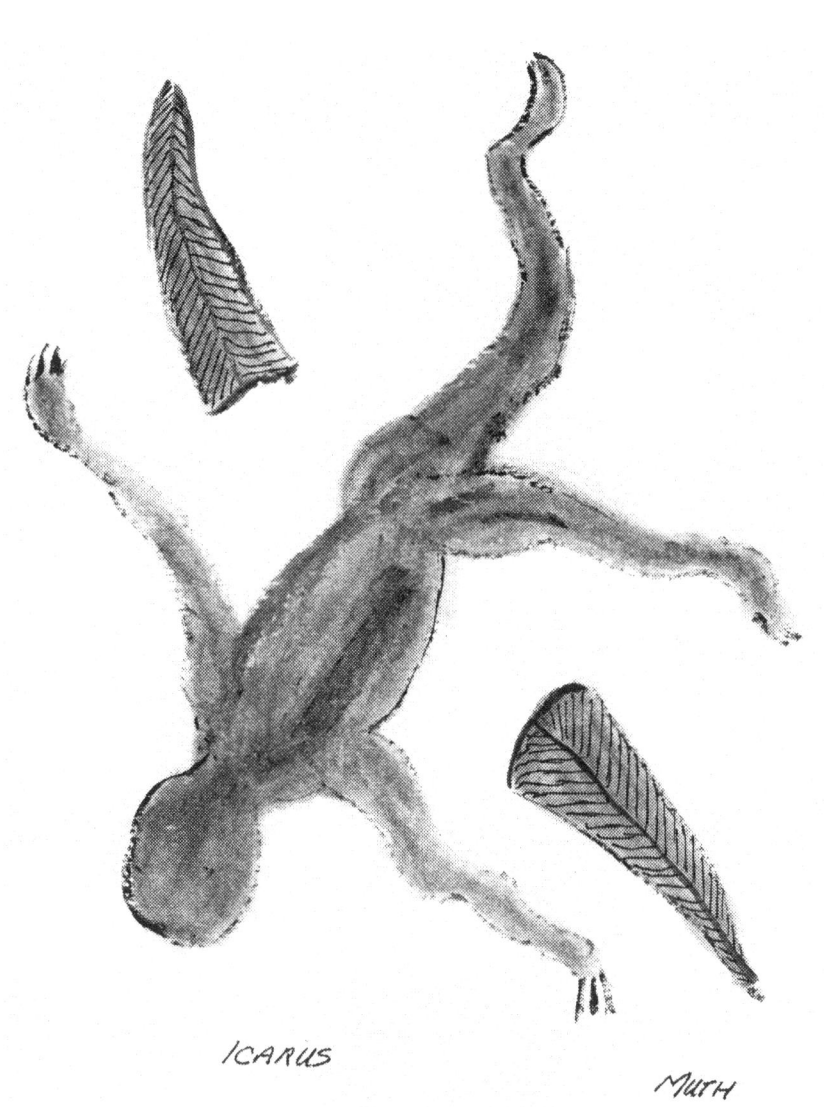

ARABESQUE

The true gracefulness of trees
Can only be seen in winter
When with limbs and branches
Curved and entwined, they stand
Posing like ballet dancers
Waiting for their music cue
To take those first steps.

Arabesque　　　Muth

PEOPLE FROM THE DREAM

Who were those people?
I visited last night in my dream
Who were those people?
Who knew my name, my face,
We had sandwiches and wine;
I saw their flowering trees,
We talked with understanding
And shared thoughts, ideas ...
Who were those people?

People From The Dream 　　　MYTH

Steve is, of course, one of my imaginary portraits,
Like many people, I have known several "Steves";
in fact, often they had to be referred to as
"Steve, the contractor," "Steve, the mailman," etc.
I don't really know who this Steve is but I imagine
him as a man who has had adventures and
interesting stories to tell.

SECOND THOUGHTS

While dusting the shelves
I pick up a seashell
Tenderly, its pure delicacy
Of shape and form
A sweet delight;
Holding it to my ear
I hear familiar sound
In childhood days
I was always told
"That is the ocean"
Later I wondered
What great sorcerer
Had imprisoned a sea
In that pink spiral
And why and how?
But now years older
There are second thoughts,
Is it the ocean or the echo
Of my own life force?

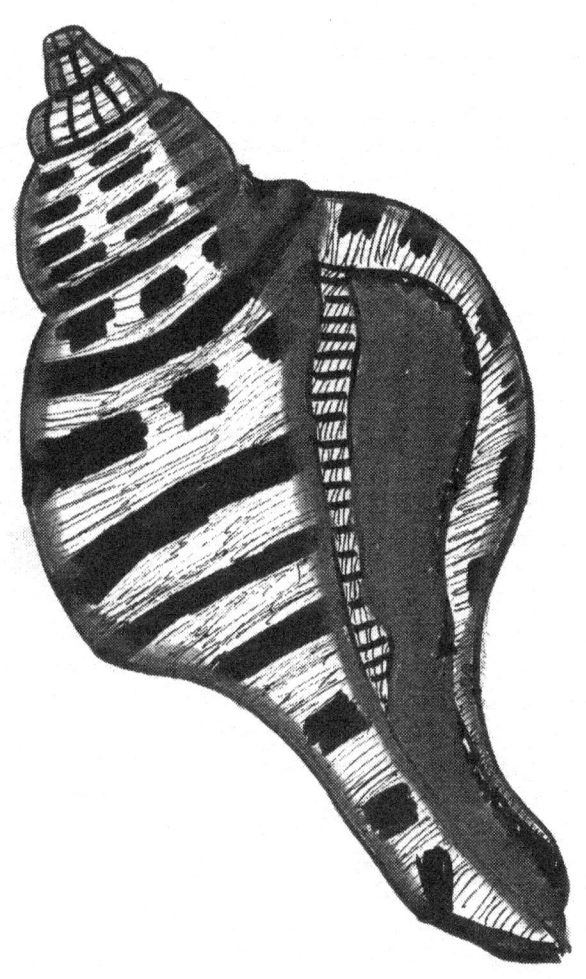

MUSIC

Music, like a fog,
Fills all the rooms;
Settles in the corners,
Creeps under the sofa
And silences all sounds
Even the clocks.

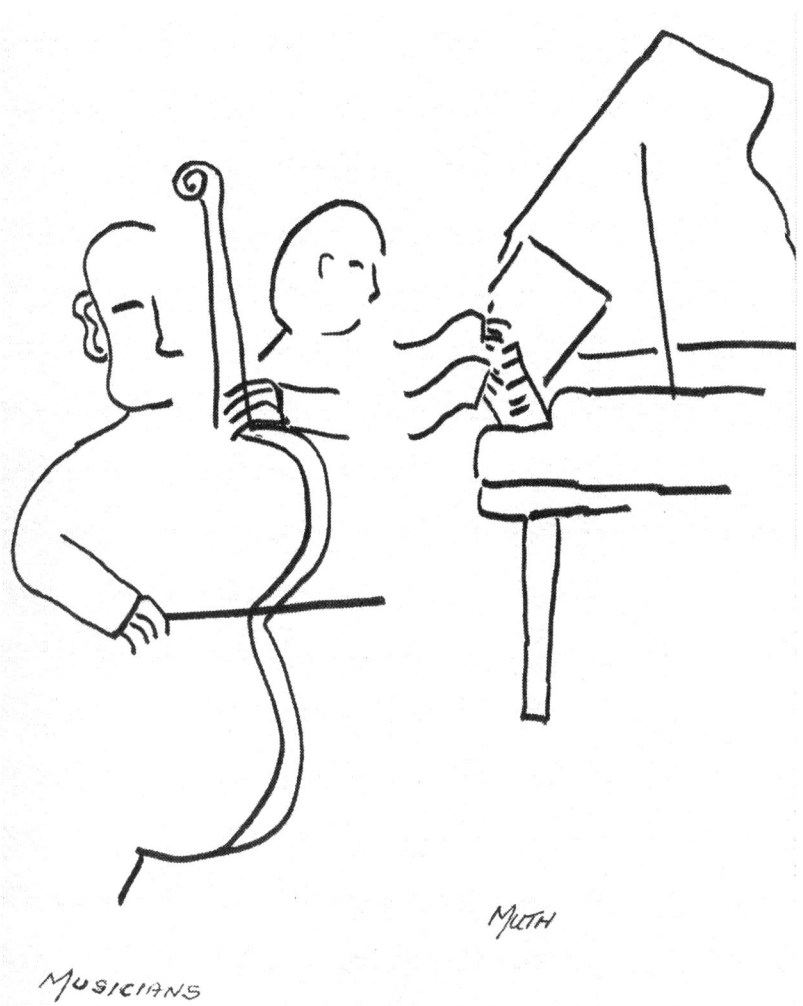

THE NUNS

I saw the nuns walking
    Close at hand
In one straight line
    Single file
Clothed in black and white
    Like a photo
From a much earlier time
    Now dimly
Buried in memory's scrapbook

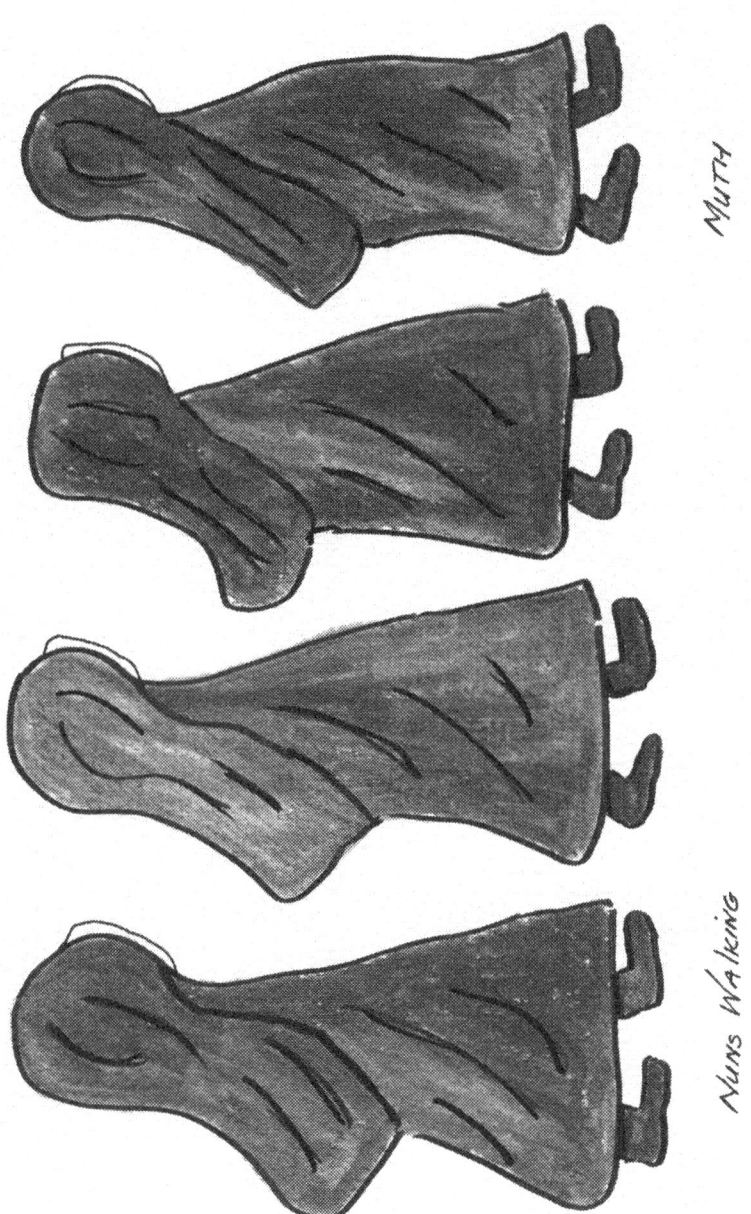

RETURN VISIT

Walking into the neighborhood of today
I find even no hints of yesterday
The streets are wider, trees gone
And the house in which I lived
Is now a sometime parking lot
Years of rain have washed away
The lettering on old brick walls
Groceries are converted to galleries
There are no children left to skate
No place left to buy ice cream cones
Whose melting sweetness was summer
But still the clouds move above
The building-punctured sky.

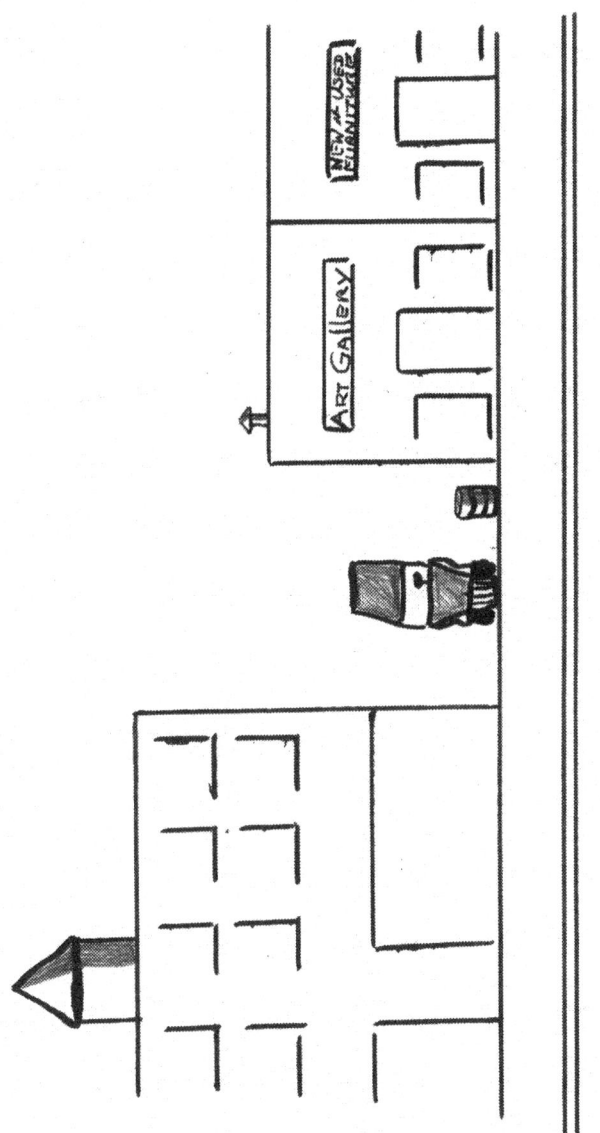

WINTER THOUGHTS

Winter is a favorite season. It is a time
of softened sounds and quietness.
It is a time for special treats like hot chocolate
and brownies. Then, too, it is a season of holidays,
family gatherings, and welcome visitors.
It means looking out at the snow
from heated warm windows.
Winter is a season of contentment.

WINTER STORM

A late winter storm
That came in the night
Not wild or boisterous
But very quiet, softened
Like a muted cello
Gives us a new view
In morning's first light;
Winter bushes filled out
With big white blossoms
While the tree branches
Tenderly cradle the snow.

WINTER AFTERNOON

Winter closes us in
With cold and clouds;
We sit by the window
Counting snowflakes,
No one comes down
The darkening road
But a rabbit pauses
By the dried bushes
And birds crowd busily
Around the feeder;
We are warm, content
But island isolated.

WINTER AFTERNOON MUTH

WINTER MORNING

The early morning winter moon
Hangs from an invisible string
In the still darkened sky
Its cold whiteness reflecting
The clumped snow in my yard
In this one quiet moment
I can hear earth's heart
Beating beneath my feet

MARCH STORM

In the late spring storm
The trees have blossomed
With wild white flowers
Short-lived but lovely,
Their snow petals melt
As the sun returns to us.

PART TWO
THE DROLLITES

The Drollites came about by accident as do so many wonderful things. I have always been a compulsive doodler. An idle moment, a bit of paper always suggested endless possibilities. This is how the Drollites came into my life. It was over twenty years ago and I was a technical writer for the Water Pollution Control Bureau and sitting in my windowless cubicle, I was trying to think up ideas for the quarterly newsletter. My mind obviously wandered from the task at hand for instead I had drawn three little figures. I liked them so much that I kept the paper and named them "Drollites." They seemed to be happy figures and the word "droll" means "amusing in an odd way" and that certainly seemed to fit. Soon they took on a life of their own, appearing in all kinds of drawings. They quickly developed an audience and became known for their love of music, art, pizza, ice cream cones and birds (including plastic pink flamingoes). I am always being asked, "Who are the Drollites?" The best answer is the one I gave when some of the drawings were in an exhibit. This is what it said:

Who ? What ? Are the Drollites ?
Some say they are from another dimension,
   or another world
At any rate from some other place.

A friend says she knows they live in the rainbow
But another friend says she saw them living
Under bridges and in caves;
I saw two in my garden last week.

Some say that Drollites are only two inches high.
But Jimmy, down the street, saw one six feet tall
And my neighbor saw one just her height—
   five feet, three inches
So I think it all depends on who you are
And where you see them.

We do know that the Drollites like people and are eager to be friends. Fortunately for me and others, the Drollites continue to thrive and enjoy their quiet adventures.

This special section is dedicated to Judith Armstrong who bought the first Drollite drawing and has been a loyal fan ever since.

The Drollites love to dance—anything from ballet, ballroom, tap-dancing to line dancing. By twos, by groups or sometimes a single Drollite can be seen tapping or twirling.

Drollites love to walk in the rain. Small Drollites like to stomp their feet in puddles.

Drollites Walking In The Rain

Singing is a specialty of the Drollites.
All of them can carry a tune. They enjoy
concerts as performers and as spectators.
It can be a friendly sing-along around
the family piano or it can be a
formal occasion with a conductor.
In this illustration, we assume that
she is singing a song by Mahler.

Not unlike us, Drollites love to have their pictures taken, especially family portraits. The family pet is included and always at least one of the youngsters acts up a bit.

Family Portrait

There are few things more delicious
and refreshing than an ice cream cone
in the summer—the cool swallow,
the crunch of the cone.

ICE CREAM CONES ON A SUMMER AFTERNOON

Weekends are a favorite time for
Drollite birdwatchers. Whole families
go out with their bird books and binoculars.

There is something magic about kite flying. Maybe it is the act of making something lift off and wander the sky. Maybe it is the age-old dream of Icarus to break free of earth's grasp.

There aren't a lot of choices of flavors but the popsicle vendor always finds eager customers. It may be that his wares are not only tasty but seem exotic to his buyers.

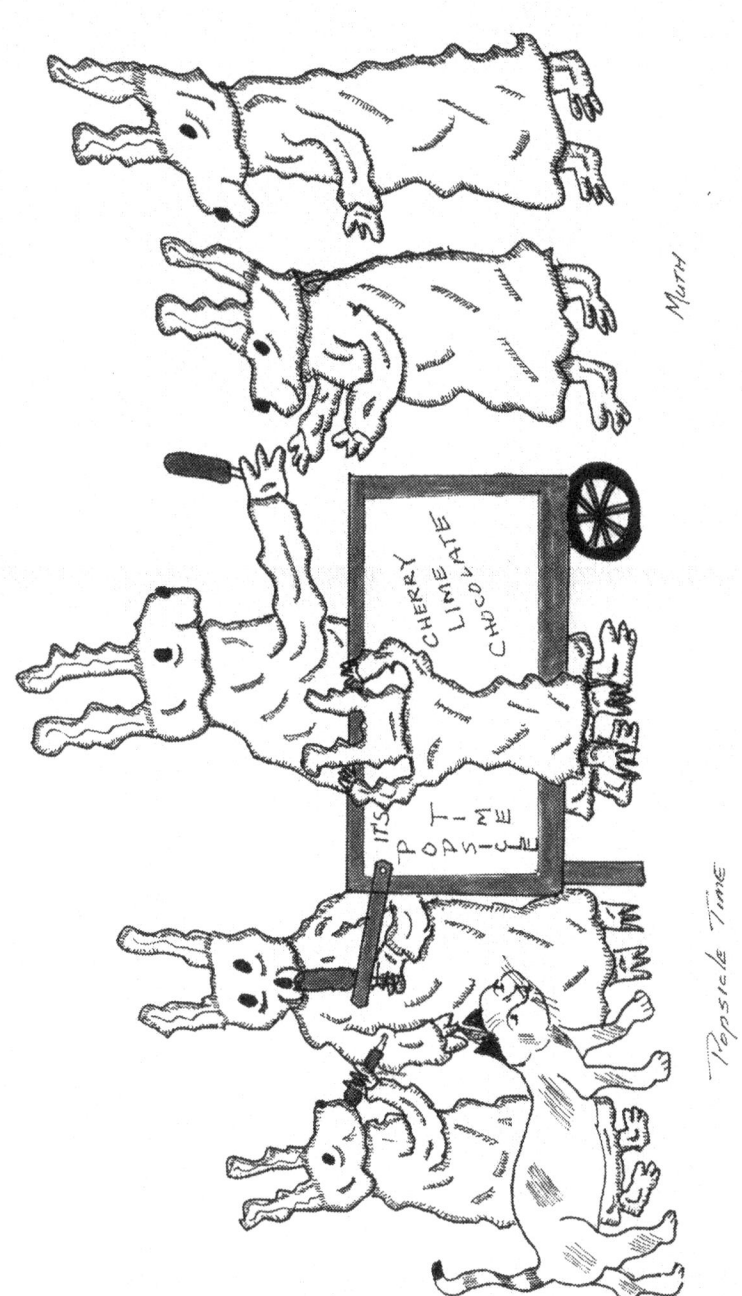

Popsicle Time

A prominent and important part of Drollite life is the circus. It is only natural that young Drollites try to emulate the performers they have seen.

ACROBATS   MUTH

Drollite jazz players can be heard everywhere, sometimes playing solos, duets, trios or in a jazz band. They love to improvise.

The Drollite Perfect Pizza Palace
lives up to its name and motto
"Every Bite Is Good."

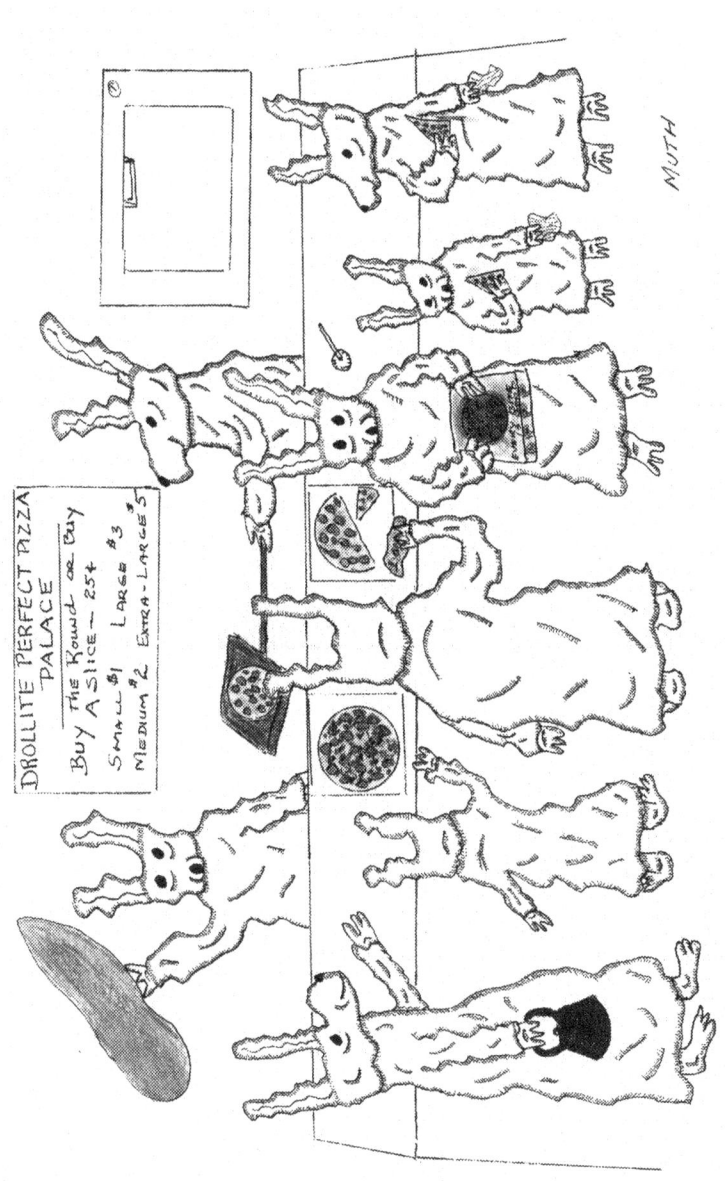

Winter fun means sledding,
making snow figures,
throwing snowballs,
building snow forts,
skating and skiing.

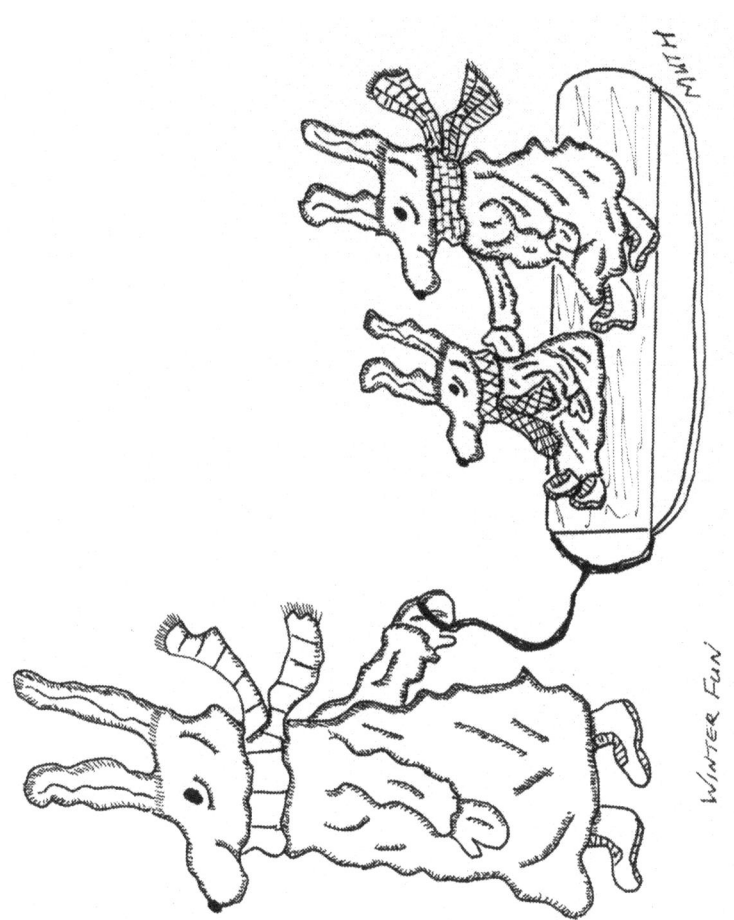

PART THREE
OTHER CREATURES

I use the term "other creatures" to designate non-human and non-Drollite beings. This includes but is not limited to small animals and birds. In fact, I also celebrate some wooden birds. The importance of creatures, real, imagined or artificial, is essential to our own human nature. What our particular role is in that relation depends upon our own personality. We are surrounded by other creatures some of which we have chosen to share our homes and lives with but others are only transient visitors. Anyone who gardens would agree with the poet James Stephens who wrote, "Little creatures, everywhere!" I am not fond of "creepy crawlies," especially spiders, but I do admire their creativity and industry. There is something special about a spider's web, delicacy and strength combined in an intricate design. While I have almost always had dogs and cats as pets, I must confess to being partial. Though both appear in my paintings, cats are my first choice when sketching. They have an easy gracefulness as well as a strong sense of self-importance. Although I have never fancied lizards as pets, I love to see them in their natural surroundings. I used to walk along a nature path that was a lizard habitat. The lizards were all ages and sizes. Some of them would quickly vanish into the brush but others would stay to stare me down. As urban sprawl continues, it is harder to get to see and know many of our fellow creatures. I feel that I was fortunate to grow up when small family farms with their animals prevailed, when the countryside was easily accessible and horse-drawn wagons were a common sight.

THE CAT FAMILY

The mother cat,
Plump with pride,
Asks for admiration
For her two kittens;
She takes all credit
Forgetting entirely
That chance encounter
In the next street.

One Cat, Two Kittens — Muth

THE FUR BAROMETER

A hint of moisture in the air
Is it rain or early snow?
In the evening it's hard to tell
What the morning light will show
Unless the cat comes in the night
Crying and with dampened fur.

CLEO, OUR CAT

Cleo hides under the blanket
The blue and white striped one
Staying there all morning
And after crunchies and milk
Slips back under in the afternoon
Where does she think she is?
In a dark but warm, quiet cave,
In a dense, safe wool forest
Or some place we can not know
Her own cat-secret dreaming space.

EARLY

In the morning cool air
Pours into the house
Puddling in the corners
Our cat finds this oasis
And settles in for a nap.

SCULPTURE

The carved birds,
Flightless in wood
Look toward the sea;
A window blocks
Their way out
But not their view.

Wooden Birds

NIGHTTIME

At dusk I hear the owl's cry
A signal for night to begin
Day birds go to their nests
Flowers turn in on themselves
Night birds seek hapless prey
Bats sally forth in group formation
The river water shines silver
Under the moon's bright glance.

RUMORS

They say
A giant lizard lives
In the unmapped area;
That uncharted green
Of the often-folded map
They say
The trees grow so tall
The sun never ever
Touches the quilted ground
They say
Somewhere in the center
Of its tangled heart
There are mighty ruins
Of a lost kingdom
They say
There are incised words
On a stone tablet
Telling of buried gold
They say
In each new generation
Some go to search
But always come back
Trembling with fear.

BLACK MASK LIZARD   MUTH

THE SUMMONS

Under the full moon
The flute sounds
Sweet, piercing notes;
Deep in his barrow
The sleeping fox
Stirs and awakes
And goes yawning
Into the night air
Answering the summons,
The call to dance
Before the ancient ones.

Fox Muth

FROM ONE ARTIST TO ANOTHER

The window glass in my bedroom
Has changed, been antiqued
By some industrious, busy spider
Weaving her web back and forth
Fastening it corner to corner.
How can I betray her trust
By washing away these strands
That are her own work of art?

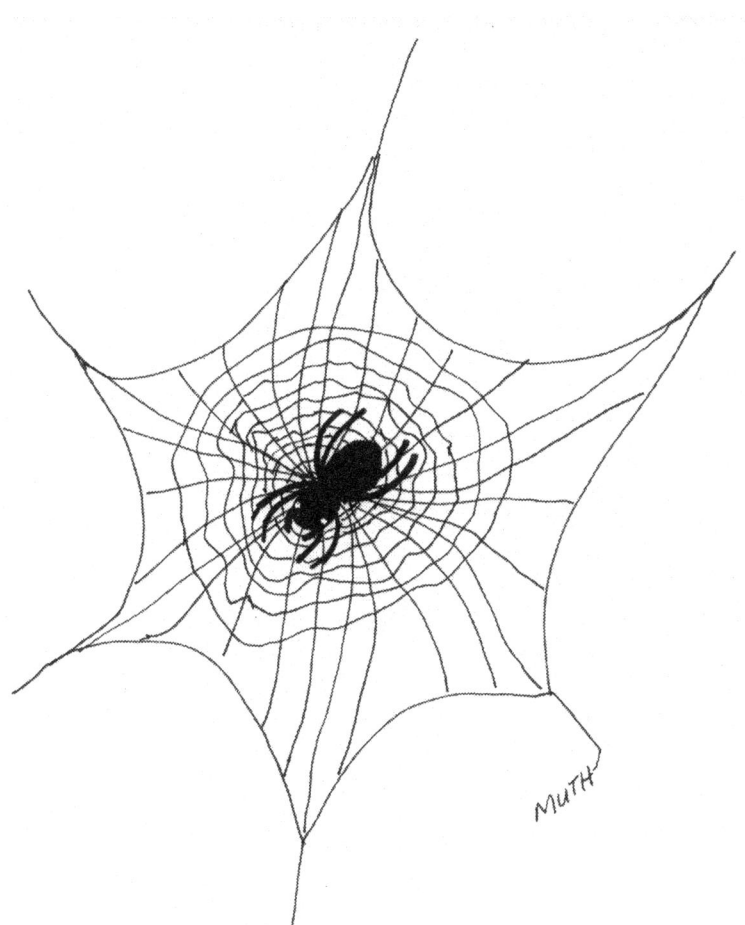

Web

ENCOUNTER

The wild hare flees from me
He does not know my gesture
Is one of only friendliness
But when I stand still, quiet
He stops also, turns around
Our eyes meet in calm communion
Then breaking the spell, he runs
Into the darker underbrush.

Wild Hare

TURTLE

The turtle crawls
Out of hiding,
Its hibernated legs
Weak, wobbly;
Spring rain washes
The winter debris
From scarred shell.
Turtle lives again
Under the summer sun.

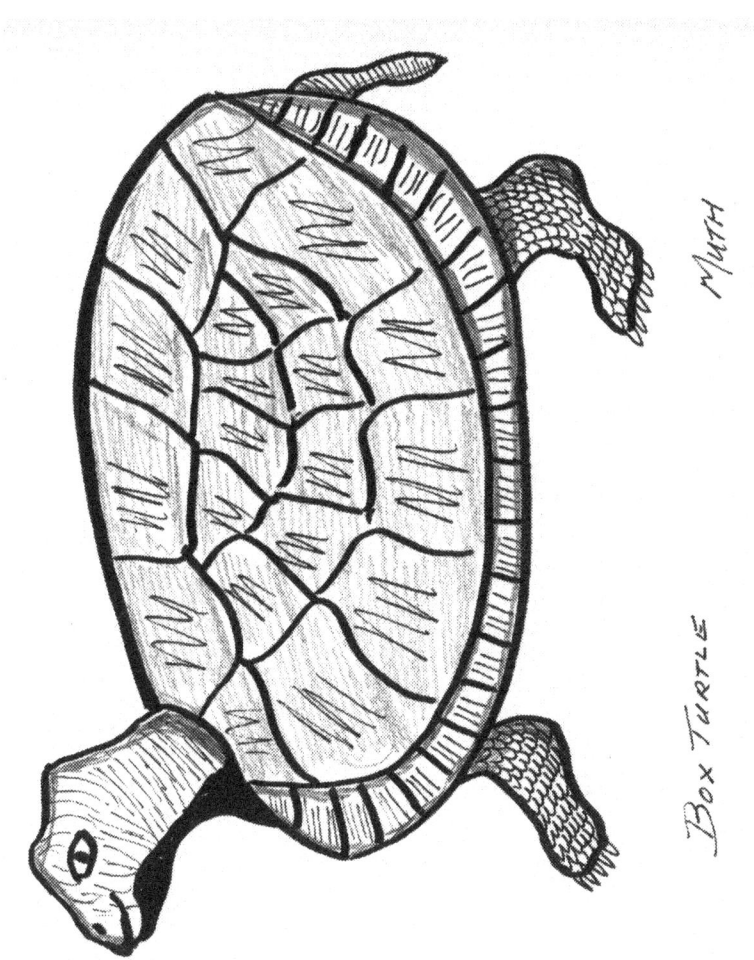

Box Turtle Myth

GHOST HORSE

I see the ghost horse
Reflected in the window
He does not gallop or run
But slowly, deliberately
Moves across the hills
He always comes at the hour
When day has just retired
And night still waits
On the doorstep, hesitant
To cast the spell of darkness.

Ghost Horse Myth

Ravens are my favorite birds and the
ones about which I most often write.
To me they seem both friendly and yet aloof,
mysterious in a sort of fairy tale way.

TOTEM BIRD

Raven is my totem bird
His harsh cry vibrates
Within my own heart,
His sleek black feathers
Whisper secrets to me
As they furl and unfurl
Wrapping around his body
Then, wings opened wide
As he flies away
My soul grasped
Firmly in his beak.

RAVEN'S CALL

I look into the trees
    For direction
A raven calls out to me
    Guide or trickster?
I am uncertain about his advice
    His invitation
To follow him down the trail
    Into the woods
And when I stop, hesitating
    He flies away
His last calls echo to the sky
    Blessing or curse?

THE MESSAGE TREE

The raven, my black-feathered guide
Flies before me, leading me to the tall tree
And while he perches on the top
I search for signs, meanings, answers;
Where shadows from bare branches form
A face, a mask, simple, subdued, silent
The sun shifts, there is change, alteration
Strange cryptic symbols scratched in bark
A word to the wise? Warning? Prophecy?
Then the raven's short, hoarse cry
Shatters the spell. He offers no clues
And when he flies away, I too leave
Having only glimpsed a hidden world.

THE INTRUDER

Suddenly the raven calls loudly
Sitting there on the telephone pole
Making it into an instant totem.
He calls again and again,
Harsh sounds in the soft air
Of this very hot summer day.
I go out to look at him, quietly
Is he predicting a coming storm
Or just reminding me of the past;
Was this once his only home?

CRITICS

The ravens walk around
The sculpture garden
Sedate, black-robed
Art critics in disguise
Now and then they pause
Gathering in noisy groups
To discuss some aspects,
Facets of construction
Form or figure design.
Finally their work done
They fly quickly away
Going in all directions
To spread their opinions.

SIGHTING

The raven appears to fly
Across the evening moon
His black wings spread out
Across the pock-marked white;
Unlike Icarus he has no fear
For the moon is still and cold
And can not scorch his wings
But he is a master of illusion
Great distance separates them
And we are once more tricked.

AUTOBIOGRAPHY

Fortified by love and poetry
    Art and music
    I am at ease
In life, numbering my days
    By the seasons
    Not the years.

INDEX OF POEMS

Arabesque, 26
Autobiography, 104

Brothers and Sisters, 18

Cat Family, The, 74
Cleo, Our Cat, 77
Credo, 11
Critics, 102

Early, 78
Encounter, 90

From One Artist To Another, 88
Fur Barometer, The, 76

Ghost Horse, 94

Icarus Revisited, 24
In the Roadside Hotel, 20
Intruder, The, 101

March Storm, 45
Message Tree, The, 100
Music, 34

Nighttime, 82
Nuns, The, 36

People From The Dream, 28

Raven's Call, 98
Return Visit, 38
River, The, 14
Rumors, 84

Sculpture, 80
Second Thoughts, 32
Sighting, 103
Sleight of Hand, 16
Sudden Rain, 22
Summons, The, 86

Totem Bird, 97
Turtle, 92

Winter Afternoon, 42
Winter Morning, 44
Winter Storm, 41
Winter Thoughts, 40

INDEX OF DRAWINGS

Acrobats, 65
Arabesque, 27

Bird Watchers, 59
Black Mask Lizard, 85
Box Turtle, 93

Conductor and The Soloist, The, 53

Dancers, 49
Dreaming Cat, 79
Drollite Perfect Pizza Palace, 69
Drollites Walking In The Rain, 51

Family Portrait, 55
Flying Owl, 83
Fox, 87

Ghost Horse, 95

Icarus, 25
Ice Cream Cones On A Summer Afternoon, 57

Jazz Notes, 67

Kite Fliers, 61

Musicians, 35

Night Clerk At The Castaway Hotel, 21
Nuns Walking, 37

Old Neighborhood, The, 39
One Cat, Two Kittens, 75

People From The Dream, 29
Popsicle Time, 63

Rainy Afternoon, 23
Raven, 99

Seated Woman/Standing Man, 19
Sleight of Hand, 17
Steve, 31

Triton, 33

Web, 89
Wild Hare, 91
Winter Afternoon, 43
Winter Fun, 71
Wooden Birds, 81